Who Cares?

An economic and ethical analysis of private
charity and the welfare state

ROBERT SUGDEN

Reader in Economics,
University of Newcastle upon Tyne

Published by
THE INSTITUTE OF ECONOMIC AFFAIRS
1983

First published in November 1983

by

THE INSTITUTE OF ECONOMIC AFFAIRS
2 Lord North Street, Westminster, London SW1P 3LB

© The Institute of Economic Affairs 1983

ISSN 0073-909X

ISBN 0-255 36167-X

Printed in Great Britain by

GORON PRO-PRINT CO LTD, LANCING, WEST SUSSEX

Set in Monotype Plantin 11 *on* 12 *point*

Contents

[3]

[4]

Preface

THE *Occasional Papers* accommodate texts that do not fit the formulae of the *Hobart Papers, Research Monographs* or other IEA series. They have been revised versions of lectures or essays that we considered should be drawn to the attention of a wider audience, or economic analyses not easily available elsewhere.

Occasional Paper 67 by Mr Robert Sugden of the University of Newcastle upon Tyne is a microcosm of a theory or explanation of giving (rather than selling) that he is developing in the academic journals and in longer texts. His work has led him to question the fashionable thinking about the rationale and benefits of 'the caring economy' institutionalised in the welfare state and its main components, the National Health Service and state education. In the course of his concise restatement in this *Occasional Paper*, Mr Sugden reviews the explanations of joint giving by compulsory taxation through the state in the writings of the late Professor R. M. Titmuss and of Professor A. J. Culyer of the University of York, with shorter references to Professors K. J. Arrow, Milton Friedman and others.

It is a common error to suppose that economists are concerned only with the economics of buying and selling in markets and not with the economics of giving and receiving in its various forms of charity and philanthropy. *The Economics of Charity*,[1] published by the IEA in 1974, was a collection of essays by 10 economists who wrote on 'the charity market', a developing department of economic analysis. (*The Price of Blood*[2] was an earlier study by Professors M. H. Cooper and Culyer of one form of giving.) Economic analysis can shed light on any activity which makes use of scarce resources that can be used in alternative ways so that their use in one way entails the sacrifice of their use in other ways. Whether they are exchanged in markets or given away, economics can show how they can do most good.

Mr Sugden's central target is the proposition that the wide-

[1] IEA Readings No. 12.
[2] Hobart Paper 41, IEA, 1968.

spread desire to express 'care' for other people, especially those 'in need', explains the emergence and persistence of the welfare state and its components. This view had been argued earlier by Professor Titmuss, though less scientifically and without the economic sophistication of Professor Culyer. The basic idea is that people who are not themselves 'in need' are willing to make gifts to those who are – but each donor is willing to give only as part of an arrangement by which *everyone* gives. Hence, it is said, voluntary giving cannot work, and the desire to give can be satisfied only through a system of taxation and public spending: the welfare state.

Mr Sugden finds this argument unacceptable, not least because it conflicts with the evidence about voluntary giving. The 'caring' approach yields plausible predictions on how much individuals will donate as their incomes vary, as tax rates change, and as the donations of other people change, but 'taken together they [the three predictions] give absurd results' (p. 25). 'The theory is self-defeating' (p. 28).

Mr Sugden goes on to discuss some alternative explanations of charity. There is, he argues, no reason to believe that private charities inevitably fail to satisfy the desires of their donors, and that some form of compulsion is called for. This undermines a central part of the 'caring economy' argument.

He also rejects the view, stated strongly by Professor Culyer, that the very existence of the welfare state is evidence for the 'caring' explanation.[1] Mr Sugden's reply to Professor Culyer is, in part, that of the public choice school of economics – that the political process is inefficient in transmitting individuals' preferences. We cannot, he says, assume that every economic arrangement that is politically approved is efficient in reflecting individual preferences: the Common Agricultural Policy is an obvious

[1] Professor Culyer says it is implausible to argue that individuals cannot convey their wishes to government. The trouble remains, especially in the supply of medical care and education, that there are no prices that inform individuals of the alternative costs of state and private services; indeed, the state specifically denies the information by supplying the services virtually without prices and by specifically denying the choice between state and private services by refusing the option of contracting out. The only effective method of discovering preferences is by attaching prices to alternative services, which has been done in a series of field surveys from 1963-78, the findings of which economists generally have ignored. (Ralph Harris and Arthur Seldon, *Over-Ruled on Welfare*, Hobart Paperback 13, IEA, 1979.)

counter-example. 'The welfare state', says Mr Sugden, 'is a mass of vested interests and any major reform would involve an immense amount of political bargaining. We cannot merely *assume* that it is efficient just as it is' (p. 33).

Moreover, Mr Sugden maintains that voters do not always record their personal preferences. They have no incentive to do so, and may instead record their general beliefs about the good of society as a whole. Thus the welfare state may reflect not 'caring' preferences but paternalistic and egalitarian beliefs expressed through the political process.

If this is true, the values that would justify the welfare state are in conflict with individual liberty – a moral dilemma the 'caring economy' approach does not recognise. Mr Sugden asks the reader, whether socialist or liberal, to face up to this conflict of values.

Mr Sugden writes clearly, and explains his terms as he goes along, but the subject requires an understanding of the central economic theory (explanation) of giving which is abstract, and a central portion of the *Paper* requires a little effort by the reader who wants to understand the important conclusions that follow Mr Sugden's argument.

The welfare state has been growing for 40 years since the Second World War, 65 years since the First World War, and 100 years or more since its beginnings in the 1870s. General Elections give no evidence of public approval, since the voter is asked to record a choice between party or coalition with 57 varieties of policies in which he cannot isolate the National Health Service, or state education, or council housing or state pensions, or any other welfare service. The welfare state now accounts for half of total government expenditure; it requires large sums in taxation; large bureaucracies organised in professional associations or trade unions that have a vested interest in even larger government expenditure and resist reform; not least, the welfare state denies choices and liberties that increasing numbers of the public might prefer. It is therefore fundamental to the course of British public policy that the justification for the welfare state should be realistically well-grounded in public behaviour, circumstances and preferences. Mr Sugden contests the dominant explanation or justification of the welfare state.

Although the Institute is required by its constitution to dissociate itself from the arguments of its authors, it presents Mr Sugden's *Occasional Paper* as a timely contribution to a public debate on essentials that should replace the attention given to warring factions that threaten to turn the British scene into a bear garden in which decisions are made by the vocal activist rather than in the interest of the general community.

October 1983   ARTHUR SELDON

The Author

ROBERT SUGDEN was born in West Yorkshire in 1949. He was educated at his local grammar school, the University of York and University College, Cardiff. He is now Reader in Economics at the University of Newcastle upon Tyne. He is the co-author (with Professor Alan Williams) of *The Principles of Practical Cost-Benefit Analysis* (Oxford University Press, 1978) and the author of *The Political Economy of Public Choice* (Martin Robertson, 1981). He has written articles about the economics of social policy and philanthropy and is currently writing a book about the ways in which people co-ordinate their behaviour in the absence of government.

Who Cares?
ROBERT SUGDEN
Reader in Economics,
University of Newcastle upon Tyne

I

ECONOMISTS AND 'CARING'

IT IS an indisputable truth that men and women sometimes sacrifice their own time and money in an effort to improve the health and welfare of others: the large number of privately-funded charitable organisations in the UK is ample evidence. Yet it may seem strange that economists should interest themselves in the study of charitable activities and motives. In popular thought, economics is still the dismal science, and its model of the individual is the rational, calculating, self-interested 'economic man'. In reality, as long as there has been economics, there have been economists interested in non-selfish behaviour. Adam Smith himself was a moral philosopher whose first book was about the 'theory of moral sentiments'. The very first sentence of that book declared that

> 'How selfish soever man may be supposed, there are evidently some principles in his nature, which interest him in the fortune of others, and render their happiness necessary to him, though he derives nothing from it except the pleasure of seeing it.'[1]

Many modern economists have studied charitable organisations and the behaviour of people who give to charities, or have thought about the implications for society of people having charitable motives.[2] There are several reasons for economists' concern with the study of charity – or, as some would say, 'caring'.

---

[1] Adam Smith, *The Theory of Moral Sentiments*, London, 1759.

[2] Examples are G. S. Becker, 'A theory of social interactions', *Journal of Political Economy*, Vol. 82, 1974, pp. 1,063-1,093; D. Collard, *Altruism and Economy*, Martin Robertson, Oxford, 1978; A. Seldon (ed.), *The Economics of Charity*, IEA Readings No. 12, IEA, 1974.

First, even in the UK today, private charities use significant amounts of resources. They have not been entirely supplanted by the welfare state, but exist alongside it, producing goods and services which people value. If economists were not able to account for this phenomenon, or were not able to predict how the extent of charitable giving would be affected by other changes, they would be failing in their task of explaining how scarce resources are allocated between competing uses. Secondly, private charities represent a partial alternative to the welfare state as a means of providing help to people in need. Many of the concerns and institutions of the modern welfare state have grown out of private charities. It is probable that, if government spending on welfare services was reduced, private philanthropy would expand to fill some of the gap. If economists had a satisfactory theory of philanthropy, they might be able to predict whether private giving would be substituted for public spending, and if so, to what extent. Thirdly, and most importantly for my present purpose, an understanding of private philanthropy might help us to understand the welfare state itself. The motives which lead people to contribute to private charities may have something in common with the motives which lead people to support the welfare state as a political principle.

Titmuss's welfare state ideology

The idea that the welfare state is associated with generosity was argued most passionately by the late Professor Richard Titmuss in his influential book, *The Gift Relationship*,[1] which studied the social institutions concerned with blood donorship and blood transfusion in a number of countries. It is a hymn of praise to the British National Blood Transfusion Service and to its guiding principle that blood should be a free gift. More generally, it is a defence of the gift relationship as an alternative to the market as a means of allocating goods. Titmuss wrote regretfully:

'We are reminded, whenever we think about the meaning of customs in historical civilisations, of how much we have lost, whatever we may have otherwise gained, by the substitution of large-scale econ-

[1] R. M. Titmuss, *The Gift Relationship*, Allen and Unwin, London, 1970.

omic systems for systems in which exchange of goods and services was not an impersonal but a moral transaction.'[1]

Significantly, however, Titmuss continually allowed the National Health Service (NHS) itself, and sometimes by extension the welfare state as a whole, to share in the moral credit of the National Blood Transfusion Service. On the first page of his text he explained that

'The study originated . . . from a series of value questions formulated in the context of attempts to distinguish the "social" from the "economic" in public policies and in those institutions and services with declared "welfare" goals. Could, however, such distinctions be drawn and the territory of social policy at least broadly defined without raising issues about the morality of society and of man's regard or disregard for the needs of others? Why should men not contract out of the "social" and act to their own immediate advantage? Why give to strangers?'[2]

This passage, I think, suggests a conviction that social policy is to be distinguished by its recognition of 'man's regard for the needs of others' and the relationship of giving. The National Blood Transfusion Service and the NHS are bracketed together as institutions based on common principles of fellowship and on 'an unspoken shared belief in the universality of need'.[3]

The importance of *The Gift Relationship* was that it offered an ideology for the welfare state. It has been popular and influential because it struck a chord in the British heart. The welfare state, and the NHS in particular, is a source of deep and genuine national pride for many British people. There is something very comforting in the belief that the NHS is not merely another nationalised industry but an embodiment of people's regard for the needs of others. My main purpose in this *Paper* will be to analyse this ideology in the cold light of economic logic. In the course of the discussion, however, I shall have a good deal to say about the economics of philanthropy.

---

[1] *Ibid.*, p. 82.   [2] *Ibid.*, p. 15.   [3] *Ibid.*, pp. 273 and 268.

II

Voluntary Giving *versus* Compulsory Taxing

At first sight, Titmuss's defence of the welfare state looks vulnerable. The welfare state does not rest on the voluntary sacrifices of private individuals. Titmuss repeatedly claimed that the true quality of giving requires that the giver should be under no compulsion to give and that he should have no expectation that his giving will induce a reciprocal gift from which he will benefit.[1] These conditions are certainly met by blood donorship in Britain, as they are by private gifts to such charities as the Spastics Society and the National Society for the Prevention of Cruelty to Children. But they are not met by the welfare state as a whole. The individual taxpayer is not free to choose whether to give financial support to the NHS or to his local social services department: he is *compelled* to pay. Further, we are all potential beneficiaries for most of the services provided by the welfare state. If I vote to be taxed to finance the welfare state, I do so on the understanding that others will be taxed also; I benefit from their payments just as they benefit from mine. In this sense, state-funded welfare services have much more in common with the police service or with the less profitable parts of British Rail than they have with private charities or with the National Blood Transfusion Service.

A clash of ideals

In addition, the ideals that Titmuss expounded so eloquently can be opposed by other ideals concerned with individual freedom. Perhaps the most famous statement of the value of freedom is in John Stuart Mill's *On Liberty*:

> 'The only purpose for which power can rightfully be exercised over any member of a civilised community, against his will, is to prevent harm to others. His own good, either physical or moral, is not a sufficient warrant. He cannot rightfully be compelled to do or forbear because it will be better for him to do so, because it will make him happier, because, in the opinion of others to do so would be wise, or even right.'[2]

[1] *Ibid.*, pp. 84-85 and 102.
[2] J. S. Mill, *On Liberty*, London, 1859, Ch. 1.

[14]

In relation to some kinds of public policy, this principle of Mill's is part of the moral equipment of millions of British people. There is, for example, a widespread aversion to the censorship of pornographic books and films (when available to adults only). The Williams Committee on Obscenity and Film Censorship not only upheld Mill's principle of liberty but also reported that most of its witnesses did the same.[1] But it is not easy to justify the welfare state without rejecting the liberal principle that each adult is the proper judge of his own welfare.

The benefits of the welfare state are mainly provided in kind rather than in cash. This is most obvious in the case of health care, but is also true of social security benefits and old-age pensions. Let us consider a person's whole lifespan viewed from the age at which he becomes an adult. The welfare state provides him, in effect, with an insurance policy and an annuity. The insurance policy gives him an entitlement to 'free' health care when he is ill, and to cash benefits contingent on sickness or unemployment. The annuity gives him an entitlement to a flow of income in old age. For these he has to pay taxes throughout his life, which he may think a good bargain. But if he does not, he is not allowed to opt out of any of the benefits of the welfare state in return for a reduction in his lifetime tax bill equivalent in value to the benefits he has chosen to forgo. (He might want to buy insurance or annuities from private companies; or he might want to do without some benefits altogether.)

Why is such contracting-out not allowed? If we really believe that each person is the proper judge of his own welfare, we cannot object that he will harm *himself* by choosing to opt out. And if the tax reduction he gains is equal to the cost of providing the benefits he forgoes, his opting out cannot harm anyone else. How, then, can anyone justify the absence of a contracting-out option without rejecting the principle that each person is the proper judge of his own welfare? Each of us, it seems, faces a moral choice. Titmuss's vision of a caring society is incompatible with Mill's vision of a free society.

[1] B. Williams, *Report of the Committee on Obscenity and Film Censorship*, Cmnd. 7772, HMSO, London, 1979.

[15]

III

The Theory of the 'Caring Economy'

In recent years a number of economists have argued that, in this matter, appearances are deceptive, and that the principles of the welfare state can be supported without rejecting principles of individual freedom. I am not concerned here with arguments which justify the welfare state by pointing to technical or practical problems in the operation of competitive markets in welfare services. (Professor Kenneth Arrow, for example, has made much of the difficulties involved in maintaining efficient competitive markets in insurance.[1]) However valid these kinds of arguments may be on their own terms, they are not satisfactory in resolving the moral conflict I have described. To interpret the welfare state as a pragmatic solution to a technical problem is to abandon the morally significant part of Titmuss's argument. To resolve the *moral* conflict we must justify the welfare state in a way that is not only free from paternalism but also able to account for the idealism of the supporters of the welfare state. We must be able to show why, in Titmuss's words, the setting up of the NHS was 'one of the most unsordid and civilised actions in the history of health and welfare policy'.[2] We must be able to show that the welfare state reflects 'man's regard for the needs of others', just as private philanthropy and blood donorship do, without at the same time denying that each person is the proper judge of his own welfare.

Friedman and state welfare

Some economists claim to have demonstrated precisely this proposition. Ironically, a particularly clear statement of this argument has been made by that tireless defender of the market system, Professor Milton Friedman. Friedman rejects all forms of paternalism and supports the market as a means of realising Mill's ideal of a free society.[3] However, in one of the most ideo-

[1] K. J. Arrow, 'Uncertainty and the welfare economics of medical care', *American Economic Review*, Vol. 53, 1963, pp. 941-973.

[2] R. M. Titmuss, *op. cit.*, p. 208.

[3] M. Friedman and R. Friedman, *Free to Choose*, Penguin Books, Harmondsworth, 1980, p. 20.

logical of his books, *Capitalism and Freedom*, after saying that there will be some poverty even in prosperous capitalist countries, he presents the following argument:

> 'One recourse, and in many ways the most desirable, is private charity. It is noteworthy that the heyday of *laissez-faire*, the middle and late nineteenth century in Britain and the United States, saw an extraordinary proliferation of private eleemosynary organisations and institutions. One of the major costs of the extension of governmental welfare activities has been the corresponding decline in private charitable activities.
>
> 'It can be argued that private charity is insufficient because the benefits from it accrue to people other than those who make the gifts . . . I am distressed by the sight of poverty; I am benefitted by its alleviation; but I am benefitted equally whether I or someone else pays for its alleviation; the benefits of other people's charity therefore partly accrue to me. To put it differently, we might all of us be willing to contribute to the relief of poverty, *provided* everyone else did. We might not be willing to contribute the same amount without such assurance.'[1]

Friedman then says that he 'accepts . . . this line of reasoning as justifying governmental action to alleviate poverty', and goes on to outline a proposal for a negative income tax.

Friedman is arguing that the relief of poverty is, in the economist's sense, a public good. A public good is consumed jointly by a group of people or by a whole community. Clean air is a classic example. The cleanliness of the air around my house is not something I can choose independently of my neighbours; we all must enjoy or suffer the same degree of cleanliness or dirtiness. When the production of public goods is left to private initiative, there is what economists call a 'free-rider problem'. Each beneficiary might be willing to contribute towards the provision of a public good in return for a promise that others would also contribute. But how can such bargains be struck if everyone has the option of refusing to join an agreement, in the hope that others will provide the public good without him? In the case of clean air, each inhabitant of a neighbourhood may be willing to burn smokeless fuel in return for a promise that all the others would do the same. But each may think that the best outcome would be for

---

[1] M. Friedman, *Capitalism and Freedom*, University of Chicago Press, Chicago, 1962, pp. 190-191.

everyone else to burn smokeless fuel while he did not. There would thus be a strong temptation to refuse to join in an agreement to burn smokeless fuel, or to break the agreement after it had been made.

In such circumstances, there is a strong argument to be made for collective rather than individual decision-making. A rule might be adopted, for example, that if a majority of householders vote for their neighbourhood to be smokeless, everyone must comply with the decision (or face legal penalties). This ground for collective decision-making contains no element of paternalism. It accepts that each person is the proper judge of his own welfare, and shows that collective decision-making can – in principle, at least – make everyone better-off. If we use *this* kind of argument to justify coercion by the state, we do not have to claim that we are wiser or more public-spirited than our fellow citizens. To put the same point in another way, when someone is compelled by law to contribute towards the cost of providing a public good, he is compelled not because it is better *for him* but because it is better *for others*.

The externalities of poverty

Friedman argues that all (or almost all) people who are relatively rich benefit from the relief of poverty. It is not entirely clear, however, what form this benefit is supposed to take. The relief of extreme poverty generates benefits which even the most hard-hearted and hard-headed can recognise – the reduction of begging, crime and social unrest, for example. The sight of poverty may also be a source of the kind of aesthetic distaste described by Professor James Buchanan:

> 'The mere fact that some members of the community are poor does not, in and of itself, normally impose an external diseconomy on many of the remaining members. What does impose such an external diseconomy is the *way* that certain people behave when they are poor. It is not the low income of the family down the road that bothers most of us: it is the fact that the family lives in a dilapidated house and dresses its children in rags that imposes on our sensibilities.'[1]

[1] J. M. Buchanan, 'What kind of redistribution do we want?', *Economica*, Vol. 35, 1968, pp. 185-190.

None of these effects of poverty, however, seems to call for the negative income tax Friedman proposes – as Buchanan himself argues. If we (the comfortably-off) want to prevent poverty from impinging on *us*, there may be many policies more effective than giving the poor money to spend as they like. We can spend more on the police; we can lock up beggars and vagrants; we can plan our towns so that the poor are confined to out-of-the-way ghettoes; we can give the poor benefits in kind, chosen so as to make their poverty as little inconvenient to us as possible. Since Friedman does not argue for this less-than-liberal approach to poverty, I think we can assume he has more generous feelings in mind when he writes of being 'distressed by the sight of poverty'; the person who is distressed really wants to help the poor, and not himself. Friedman seems to be arguing that, *for altruistic reasons*, people prefer their fellows not to suffer from extreme want. Private charities have emerged in response to this preference, but they cannot be wholly successful because of the free-rider problem. Thus, he concludes, governmental action to alleviate poverty is justified.

This kind of argument need not be restricted to justifying the provision of a minimum level of income support (though Friedman would no doubt be unhappy to see it extended much beyond this). It can be used to justify most of the activities of the welfare state. All that is required is the assumption that people have the appropriate kinds of altruistic preferences.

Arrows's 'interdependencies' . . .

Professor Arrow has marshalled the same argument. In an influential paper about the economics of medical care, he first points out that the control of communicable diseases is a public good. This is indisputable, although only a small part of public expenditure on medical care is devoted to such diseases. But, he continues:

> 'Beyond this special area there is a more general interdependence, the concern of individuals for the health of others . . . In interdependencies generated by concern for the welfare of others there is always a theoretical case for collective action if each participant derives satisfaction from the contributions of all.'[1]

[1] K. J. Arrow, *op. cit.*, p. 954.

[19]

Professor A. J. Culyer has deployed this kind of argument particularly effectively as a means of simultaneously explaining and justifying the NHS. As he states in the final sentence of his book, *Need and the National Health Service*, his aim is 'rationally to persuade the unconvinced of the NHS's necessity, as well as rallying the faithful to stand by the ideals of the NHS as they really are'.[1] His thinking is set out in more detail in another of his books, *The Political Economy of Social Policy*.[2]

Professor Culyer's fundamental assumption is that people care about one another. Each person, he asserts, typically prefers his fellow citizens to enjoy more rather than less health care, or better rather than worse health. (It is important for Culyer's argument that people should care about other people's *health*, rather than about their welfare in general. If we all cared only about one another's general welfare, and if no-one questioned anyone else's competence to look after himself, it might be possible to build a public-good argument for providing income support for the poor; but it would not be possible to justify institutions like the NHS, which provide benefits in kind.) Given this assumption, each person's health is a public good, providing benefits not only to the person directly concerned but also to his caring neighbours. If the provision of health services were left to private initiative, too little would be supplied because of the kind of free-rider problem described by Friedman. Thus, Culyer claims, there is a *prima facie* case for governmental intervention in the market for health care. This does not necessarily mean that the state must *produce* health services, as in Britain; a compulsory insurance scheme might be sufficient. But some compulsion to pay for health services is an understandable and justifiable response to the free-rider problem.

This sort of argument is attractive to many people because it offers a solution to the moral conflict described earlier. If it is correct, we may advocate compulsory health insurance or a tax-financed health service, without denying that each person is the

---

[1] A. J. Culyer, *Need and the National Health Service*, Martin Robertson, London, 1976, p. 151.

[2] A. J. Culyer, *The Political Economy of Social Policy*, Martin Robertson, Oxford, 1980.

proper judge of his own welfare. Similarly, we may advocate tax-financed unemployment benefits and old-age pensions. It is true that these policies all impose constraints on individuals' choices; for example, I am not free to convert my entitlement to health care into cash. But this constraint is necessary, not to prevent me from harming myself, but rather to prevent me from harming others. The others in this instance are my caring neighbours who, for altruistic reasons, prefer that I should enjoy good health. The harm may be an unusual kind of harm; but it is harm nonetheless. Thus there seems to be no conflict with the principle of freedom espoused by Mill.

Further, this argument explains and justifies the welfare state by employing the concepts of giving and caring. Because of this, it can account for the idealism of the welfare state's supporters; what they are supporting is not an ordinary nationalised industry but (in Culyer's words) 'a kind of national charity'[1] – or, more grandly, a 'caring economy'.[2] Even though contributions to this charity are compulsory, it exists in response to the same selfless motives as lie behind blood donations and private philanthropy. We can take pride in the welfare state because it shows that we live in a society where people care for one another. If the argument is valid, Titmuss's inspiring rhetoric really is grounded in economic logic.

IV

PRIVATE PHILANTHROPY AND THE WELFARE STATE

Is IT correct to view the various activities of the welfare state as 'national charities'? Do we really live in the kind of 'caring economy' that Professors Arrow and Culyer – and indeed Friedman – describe? One way of trying to answer these questions is to analyse private philanthropy, to find out how people behave when they give to charities.

The theory of the 'caring economy' rests on a particular ex-

---

[1] *Need and the National Health Service, op. cit.*, p. 91.
[2] 'The Caring Economy' was the title Professor Culyer chose for a public lecture at the University of Otago in 1979.

planation of private charity. The case for public provision of welfare services begins from the assumption that these services are public goods because of people's altruistic or 'caring' preferences. The state has to take action to ensure that public goods are provided in adequate quantities because, so the argument goes, private action will always fall foul of the free-rider problem. In Friedman's words (quoted above, p. 17), private charity is 'insufficient'. We might all of us be willing to contribute more than we do if only we could be sure that everyone else would do the same; and we need the coercive power of government to provide such an assurance.

But how do we *know* that private charity is insufficient? Those economists who advance this proposition do not provide any direct evidence in support. What they offer instead is a *theoretical* argument. They propose a specific theory of the workings of private charity and then show that the theory *predicts* insufficient supply. I shall argue that this 'public-good theory of philanthropy' is inconsistent with the evidence and must therefore be rejected. The argument that follows is presented more technically in a recent paper of mine in the *Economic Journal*.[1]

The public-good theory of philanthropy

The public-good theory of philanthropy can be explained by way of a simple 'model'. (This model is not my invention; it has been used by several proponents of the theory, including Professors Robert Schwartz[2] and Gary Becker.[3]) Let us suppose that all the usual consumer goods are collapsed into one, called 'private consumption', and also that all charitable activities are collapsed into one. Let us further suppose that both private consumption and the charitable activity can be measured in money (if we are concerned with the kind of charity which appeals for gifts of money, there is no harm in treating its total income as a measure of the extent of its activities). Finally, let us suppose that the charitable activity is financed entirely from voluntary contri-

[1] R. Sugden, 'On the economics of philanthropy', *Economic Journal*, Vol. 92, 1982, pp. 341-350.

[2] R. A. Schwartz, 'Personal philanthropic contributions', *Journal of Political Economy*, Vol. 78, 1970, pp. 1,264-1,291.

[3] G. S. Becker, *op. cit.*

butions, so that its income is equal to the total contributions of all philanthropists.

According to the theory, only two things matter to each philanthropist: his own consumption, and the total income of the charity. He is *not* directly concerned about the size of his own contribution; he is concerned about it only indirectly, to the extent that it affects his private consumption and the charity's total income. As Friedman puts it, the person who is distressed by the sight of poverty is benefitted equally whether he or someone else pays for its alleviation. This assumption is crucial because, without it, the charitable activity would not be a public good and the free-rider problem could not arise.

The theory further assumes that each philanthropist takes everyone else's contribution as given, that is, as outside his control or influence, and chooses his own contribution so as to bring about the final outcome he most prefers. Let us suppose, for example, that my income is £10,000 a year and that I am considering how much to contribute to a charity. I know the charity's income from other donors is £20,000 a year. If I give nothing at all, therefore, I shall spend £10,000 on private consumption and the charity will spend £20,000. If I give £1, I shall spend £9,999 on myself while the charity spends £20,001. And so on. I have to decide which of all the combinations of private consumption and charitable spending I most prefer, and then make the appropriate contribution.

At first sight, this theory seems to work quite well. It makes three predictions, two of which we know to be true and a third which, while not yet adequately tested, does not seem implausible.

Prediction 1: more income = more giving

The first prediction is that a rise in a person's income will cause him to contribute more to charity. This prediction follows from the normal assumption of economics that, as a person's income rises, he buys more of all goods. In the theory, there are only two 'goods', private consumption and the charitable activity. To say that the philanthropist 'buys' more of both when his income increases is to say that he gives some part, but not all, of any increase in income to charity. This expectation is borne out by all the evidence. A number of studies have been made – mostly

[23]

in North America – of the relationship between income and charitable giving. All have found that richer people give more than poorer people. Roughly speaking, each 1 per cent increase in income generates an increase in donations of between 0·4 and 0·8 per cent.[1,2]

Professor David Collard has attempted a similar analysis for the UK, although he admits that the data available here are 'highly treacherous'. He found a similar effect at work: each 1 per cent increase in income generated an increase in donations of about 0·7 per cent.[3]

Prediction 2: higher marginal tax rate = more giving

The second prediction of the theory requires a slight modification to the model. Let us suppose that contributions to charity can be offset against income tax (this is standard practice in the US, whereas in the UK *covenanted* gifts can be offset against tax but one-off gifts cannot). Then a sacrifice of less than £1 on the part of the donor is sufficient to ensure that the charity receives £1. If, for example, income is taxed at the rate of 30 per cent, I can benefit a charity by £1 while sacrificing only 70 pence; the 'price of giving' may be said to be 0·7. It is one of the most fundamental principles of economics that, as the price of a good falls, the quantity demanded rises. In the case of charity, the price of giving falls if gifts are exempted from tax; and, if they are exempted, it also falls as the rate of tax increases. Thus, other things equal, we would expect people to give more[4] to charity the higher their

[1] R. A. Schwartz, *op. cit.*; M. Feldstein and A. Taylor, 'The income tax and charitable contributions', *Econometrica*, Vol. 44, 1976, pp. 1,201-1,222; R. D. Hood, S. A. Martin and L. S. Osberg, 'Economic determinants of individual charitable donations in Canada', *Canadian Journal of Economics*, Vol. 10, 1977, pp. 653-669; M. J. Boskin and M. Feldstein, 'Effects of the charitable deduction on contributions by low-income and middle-income households', *Review of Economics and Statistics*, Vol. 59, 1977, pp. 351-354; C. T. Clotfelter, 'Tax incentives and charitable giving', *Journal of Public Economics*, Vol. 13, 1980, pp. 319-340.

[2] Perhaps surprisingly, charity is not a luxury good; richer people seem to give away smaller proportions of their incomes than poorer people, after allowance is made for the higher marginal tax rates faced by richer people.

[3] D. Collard, *op. cit.*, pp. 93-96.

[4] 'More' here refers to the amount the charity receives, not the sacrifice the donor makes.

marginal rate of tax. This expectation is also borne out by American investigations, which have invariably found that gifts increase as the price of giving falls. Most investigators have found that each 1 per cent fall in the price of giving produces an increase in gifts of more than 1 per cent,[1] which implies that tax exemption not only makes charities better-off but also leads people to sacrifice more of their own consumption.

Prediction 3: giving more when others give less

The third prediction of the theory is that each philanthropist will give *more* the *less* income the charity receives from other people. A reduction in the charity's income from others has the same effect on the philanthropist as a reduction in his own income: both restrict the combinations of private consumption and charitable activity he can afford. We would expect him to 'buy' less of both 'goods' in either instance. But in saying that he 'buys' less of the charitable activity, we mean that he allows the *total* income of the charity to fall. If his own consumption falls, *his* contribution to the charity must increase. The prediction, therefore, is that, if other people contribute £1 less, the philanthropist will contribute more, but not as much as an extra £1.

This prediction is much more difficult to test than the others. We can test the first prediction – that gifts increase with income – by comparing the gifts of people with different incomes. Similarly, we can test the second prediction by comparing the gifts of people facing different tax rates. But we cannot easily compare the gifts of people with different values of 'total contributions by other people'. In a large community, 'total contributions by everyone but Smith' and 'total contributions' are almost the same; and, obviously, everyone faces the same total. I know of no satisfactory test of the hypothesis that each person's gifts are inversely related to those of everyone else.

As long as we examine these predictions in isolation, the public-good theory of philanthropy seems quite satisfactory. Taken together, however, they give absurd results. Let us consider the *combined* effect of a £1 increase in a philanthropist's income and a

---

[1] Feldstein and Taylor, *op. cit.*; Boskin and Feldstein, *op. cit.*; W. S. Reece, 'Charitable contributions: new evidence on household behaviour', *American Economic Review*, Vol. 69, 1979, pp. 142-151.

£1 decrease in the income of the charity from other people. For simplicity, let us suppose gifts are *not* tax-deductible. The theory predicts that the philanthropist's gift must increase by exactly £1. Why?

Returning to a previous example, let us suppose my income is £10,000 a year and the charity's total income is £20,000 a year. I can choose to give any amount between zero and £10,000. In other words, I can choose any combination of private consumption and charitable activity subject to two conditions. First, the total value of private consumption and charitable activity must be £30,000. Secondly, private consumption must not be more than £10,000.

Let us now suppose my income rises to £10,001 and the charity's income from other people falls to £19,999. What combinations of private consumption and charitable activity are open to me now? I can choose any combination with a total value of £30,000, provided private consumption is no higher than £10,001. Provided I always give at least £1, *the options available to me are exactly the same as before*. Let us suppose that, in the first case, I chose to give £10. Then the charity would finish up with £20,010 and I would have £9,990 left for myself. This option is still available to me in the second case, so there is no reason for me not to choose it again. But now, if I want the charity to finish up with £20,010, I have to give £11, that is, I have to give away the whole of my £1 increase in income to counteract the charity's loss of income from other people.

There must therefore be a particular relationship between, on the one hand, the extent to which I give more as *my* income increases and, on the other, the extent to which I give more as *the charity's* income falls. Let us suppose I give 10p more for every £1 increase in my income. If the public good theory of philanthropy is right, a £1 rise in my income, combined with a £1 decrease in the charity's, will lead me to increase my gift by £1. So I must give 90p more for every £1 fall in the charity's income. Similarly, if I give 5p more for every £1 rise in my income, I must give 95p more for every £1 fall in the charity's income. And so on.[1]

This prediction does not seem to have been noticed by the proponents of the public-good theory. It is surely most implaus-

---

[1] I am still leaving aside the complication of tax exemption.

ible. I invite the reader to carry out a mental experiment. Consider any large charity you support, and guess its current annual income from sources other than your gifts. Suppose you are told your guess is exactly correct. How much would you continue to give to the charity in a year? Now suppose, instead, that the charity's income is £10 more than your original guess. How much *less* would you give? Call your answer X. Next, suppose your annual income increases by £10. How much *more* would you give to the charity in a year? Call your answer Y. Now add X and Y. According to the public-good theory, the total should be exactly £10. I should be very surprised if your total is more than £1.

An implausible hypothesis

Is there *evidence* to refute this prediction of the public-good theory? We know that charitable giving tends to increase less than proportionately as income increases (above, pp. 23-24). So the 'marginal propensity to give' (the proportion of any *increase* in income that is given to charity) is less than the 'average propensity to give' (the proportion of *total* income given to charity). Since by far the largest part of almost any household's income is devoted to private consumption, we can be sure that the marginal propensity to give is quite small; for an average household, a value of 5 per cent would probably be an over-estimate.[1]

As already explained, it is difficult to get direct evidence about the relationship between one person's gifts and those of other people. But it is scarcely plausible to suppose that a typical donor would give 95p more for every £1 fall in the income of, say, the Cancer Research Campaign – whose annual income is measured in millions of pounds. If donors really behaved like that, there would be some rather odd consequences. Let us suppose that Bloggs, the rich philanthropist, suddenly decides to give £10,000 a year to a charity which has 1,000 regular donors. Each of these donors will cut back his own contribution in response to Bloggs's action. (This effect will be tempered by another: each donor will increase his own contribution in response to the others' reductions.) If we assume (optimistically from the charity's point of view) that the marginal propensity to give is 5 per cent, it turns

[1] R. Sugden, *op. cit.*, pp. 347-348.

out that Bloggs's £10,000 donation ultimately benefits the charity by approximately 53 pence![1] The theory is self-defeating. Bloggs's motive for giving is to benefit the charity. Yet if he understood the consequences of his act, he would know that the charity will hardly benefit at all.

What is wrong with the theory? The fault can be traced to the fundamental assumption that the philanthropist is not directly concerned about his own contribution to a charity but only about his private consumption and the charity's total income. As far as he is concerned, *his* gift is no more significant, pound for pound, than anyone else's; he 'is benefitted equally, whether he or someone else pays'.[2] An increase in his own income is no more significant to him than the same increase in the charity's income. This implausible hypothesis produces the theory's strange predictions. *But it is also the hypothesis which provides the starting point for the 'caring economy' explanation of the welfare state.* If we reject that hypothesis, we must reject the 'caring economy' model too.

V

EXPLAINING PRIVATE CHARITY

IF WE reject the public-good theory of philanthropy, what are we to put in its place? I think our starting point must be the recognition that a philanthropist *does* distinguish between his own gifts and those of other people. He is concerned about how much *he* helps a charitable cause, and not merely about the extent of the charitable activity *as a whole*. The *act* of giving has a moral significance over and above the significance of its direct consequence.

Some economists have considered this possibility. Usually, however, they have suggested that people give to charity as a

---

[1] The charity finishes up 53 pence better off. Each of the regular donors gives approximately £10.00 less than before so that, as far as any one of them is concerned, the charity's income from everyone else has increased by £10.53. This leads each to reduce his own gift by 95 per cent of £10.53, which is £10.00. More detailed calculations are in my paper, 'On the economics of philanthropy', *op. cit.*

[2] M. Friedman, above, p. 17.

means of gaining the approval of their fellows, or of avoiding their disapproval. Professor Becker, for example, thinks the public-good theory is the most satisfactory explanation of philanthropy, but he concedes that people might derive satisfaction from the act of giving itself. This, he says, leads to 'apparent "charitable" activity . . . motivated by a desire to avoid the scorn of others or to receive social acclaim'.[1] The implication is that such behaviour is not really charitable at all.

The idea of social acclaim is, however, a red herring. We cannot explain why people behave morally merely by supposing they want others to see them doing right. *Some* people may behave morally merely to gain the approval of their fellows. But to suppose that *everyone* does so is to give no explanation of moral behaviour at all. Let us suppose I am entirely self-interested, but that I give to the NSPCC to improve my standing with my friends. Why does this improve my standing, if not because they believe I *ought* to give? If they too were entirely self-interested, and thought it entirely right for everyone to pursue his own interests to the exclusion of everything else, why would they admire me for being so stupid as to give money away? To put it another way, when I give to the NSPCC I am faking; I am pretending to be motivated by concern for the welfare of children. But there cannot be fakes without genuine articles. Apparent charitable activity is impossible unless there is real charitable activity too. We still need to explain the real thing.

A theory of private philanthropy: first steps

Economics has a long way to go before it has a fully satisfactory theory of private philanthropy. Some first steps have, however, been made. One of the most promising lines of inquiry is to suppose that people are taught, and believe, that free-riding is morally wrong; moral rules have evolved which instruct us to contribute a fair share to the production of public goods. Some economists, including Professor Collard,[2] have suggested that people act out of the so-called 'Kantian' motive.[3] Each person

[1] G. S. Becker, *op. cit.*, p. 1,083.　　[2] *Altruism and Economy, op. cit.*

[3] Named after the German philosopher Immanuel Kant (1724-1804). Kant argued that, to behave morally, a person must act only on maxims that he could will to be general laws. Collard's 'Kantian motive' is an adaptation of Kant's more general prescription.

[29]

carries out a mental experiment. He assumes that everyone else will contribute exactly as much as he does, and then decides what contribution would be best for him *on this assumption*. He is morally obliged to make this contribution, irrespective of what the others actually do. This is the 'Kantian' principle. Alternatively, it might be said that he is morally obliged to make this contribution only if the others do the same. This is the 'principle of reciprocity'. I believe that a good deal of philanthropy may be explained in terms of reciprocity.[1]

This branch of economics is still in its infancy and it is far too early to say how successful it will prove. But we should be suspicious of any claim that the free-rider problem is *never* overcome by voluntary action. If private philanthropy succeeds in supplying significant amounts of a public good, we should not *automatically* assume that the amounts are insufficient and that everyone would benefit from the replacement of private charity by public compulsion.

VI

EXPLAINING THE WELFARE STATE

THE PROPONENTS of the 'caring economy' hypothesis claim that it explains the existence of the welfare state. If their theory is wrong, some other explanation is required. Some of them, however, go further and write as if no other explanation were possible. The very existence of the welfare state is taken as evidence that the 'caring' hypothesis is true.

Professor Arrow uses this argument in the passage quoted in part earlier:

'Beyond this special area there is a more general interdependence, the concern of individuals for the health of others. The economic manifestations of this taste are to be found in individual donations

---

[1] The principle of reciprocity is a variant of the 'principle of fairness' proposed by H. L. A. Hart in his paper 'Are there any natural rights?', *Philosophical Review*, Vol. 64, 1955, pp. 175-191. The idea of reciprocity is one of the main themes of a book I am currently writing (to be published by Martin Robertson).

to hospitals and to medical education, as well as in the widely accepted responsibilities of government in this area.'[1]

Arrow is pointing here to two kinds of evidence in support of the 'caring economy' hypothesis. The first concerns private giving to medical charities (he is referring to the USA, where this sort of philanthropy is much more significant than in the UK). I have already considered and rejected this sort of evidence. The second kind is simply that democratically-elected governments provide subsidised or free medical care, or institute compulsory health insurance schemes. From this evidence Arrow infers that these responsibilities of government are 'widely accepted'.

Why are these observations evidence for the 'caring economy' hypothesis? The logic behind Arrow's claim is spelt out more fully by Culyer in an argument which is both simple and, at first sight, devastating:

> 'The very *existence* of the Welfare State is evidence for the proposition that specific caring exists, for if individuals did not care for one another then no externality would exist and there would be little reason for collectivist action . . .
>
> 'Of course it is open to anyone to deny the relevance of this evidence. One could assert . . . that the size and composition of the public sector are not the response of rational individuals to a commonly experienced externality of the sort we have postulated but are the product of years of deceit by power-seeking politicians who have convinced their electors that they really can "have something for nothing". Or one may suppose instead that the electors have foolishly not understood the lessons of economics and the results are all a dreadful mistake.
>
> 'However, both the assumption that individuals are *persistently* conspired against without discovery and the assumption that they *persistently* fail to convey their (perfectly rational) wishes to government are assumptions that are not normally invoked in economics – nor indeed in any social science – and seem, on the face of it, more implausible than the alternative.'[2]

The argument may be re-stated thus. The welfare state provides benefits in kind rather than in cash. If people's preferences were entirely selfish, this policy would be economically inefficient. If

[1] K. J. Arrow, *op. cit.*, p. 954.
[2] A. J. Culyer, *The Political Economy of Social Policy*, *op. cit.*, pp. 65-67.

people were allowed the option of taking the benefits of the welfare state in the form of cash, those who refused the option would be no worse-off than before, while those who took it would, in their own estimation, be better-off. The cost to the taxpayer would remain the same. Thus someone who rejects the assumptions of the 'caring economy' theory has to argue that, by means of a change of public policy, it would be possible to make some people better-off without making any others worse-off. But, says Culyer, this is a most implausible claim. If this change in policy would have such obviously desirable consequences, why has it not been carried out long ago? If everyone stands to gain from the dismantling of the welfare state, why does it still exist?

Individual preferences and the political process

Arrow and Culyer are making a very strong assumption about the workings of democratic institutions. They are assuming that the outcomes of the political process are never 'Pareto-inefficient'.[1] It should be noted that they do not make the same claim about behaviour *outside* politics. When a public good is involved, they argue that voluntary individual action *will* lead to a Pareto-inefficient outcome – that it would be possible to benefit everyone by producing more of the public good and paying for it by compulsory taxation. They accept that the people in this Pareto-inefficient situation are not being conspired against or failing to convey their wishes to one another; each is behaving perfectly rationally in his own terms when he takes a free ride. It is, they judge, merely an unfortunate characteristic of the game being played that rational behaviour by every individual can lead to an inefficient outcome. Might not the same be true of the political game?

This question is central to the theory of 'public choice'. Public choice economists like Professors James Buchanan, Gordon Tullock and Geoffrey Brennan have shown that there is every reason to doubt the efficiency of the political process.[2]

[1] In economic jargon, an outcome is Pareto-inefficient or 'economically inefficient' if it is possible to make a change that would benefit some people and harm none.

[2] J. M. Buchanan and Gordon Tullock, *The Calculus of Consent*, University of Michigan Press, Ann Arbor, 1962; G. Brennan and J. M. Buchanan, *The*
[*Contd. on p. 33*]

Quite apart from the theory of public choice, however, economists have always been ready to propose reforms which would increase economic efficiency; and they have never taken the failure of their advocacy as proof that they were wrong. Most economists, for example, would argue that the EEC's Common Agricultural Policy is grossly inefficient. In principle, it would be possible to reform it without harming any major interest group; those who benefit from the CAP could be bought off with special subsidies. The problem is to negotiate the price at which a vested interest can be bought off; in EEC politics, such haggling could take years. The continued existence of the CAP is not compelling evidence that it is, after all, efficient. National politics is also about negotiation. The welfare state is a mass of vested interests and any major reform would involve an immense amount of political bargaining. We cannot merely *assume* that it is efficient just as it is.

Preferences and social welfare judgements

Arrow and Culyer's argument also assumes that, when people vote, *they record their personal preferences.* There is, however, an important distinction to be made between a person's *preferences* and his *judgements about social welfare* (or about the public interest). Let us suppose, for example, that someone were to propose a minimum salary of £100,000 a year for university teachers, together with complete security of employment for all holders of tenured posts in universities. I should certainly *prefer* this proposal to the *status quo*, but I could not sincerely say that I believed it would increase *social* welfare, or be in the public interest. If (and this strains credulity) a referendum were to be taken on this proposal, I should have to decide whether to vote in accordance with my personal preferences or in accordance with my judgement of the public interest.

In the passage quoted above (p. 31), Culyer simply ignores the possibility that people might, when voting, record their social welfare judgements rather than their preferences. It is not in-

[*Contd. from p. 32*]
  Power to Tax, Cambridge University Press, 1980; A. Seldon (ed.), *The Economics of Politics*, IEA Readings No. 18, IEA, 1978; and Tullock, *The Vote Motive*, Hobart Paperback No. 9, IEA, 1976.

[33]

consistent for someone to say: 'I know that dismantling the welfare state would benefit me, and I should prefer this policy to the *status quo*. But because I believe that the welfare state serves the public interest, I shall vote for its continued existence'. Such a voter is not being 'conspired against' by 'power-seeking politicians'. Nor is he 'failing to convey his wishes' to the government.

There is a long tradition of belief that people *ought*, when voting, to record their judgement of the public interest rather than their private preferences.[1] This tradition might be expected to have had some influence on how people vote.[2] Furthermore, the political system offers no incentives for people to record their own preferences. A cynic might say: 'It is all very well for people to have high ideals about the public interest but, when it comes to the point, self-interest will prevail'. In a typical election, however, the influence of an individual's vote is so tiny as to be negligible. Self-interest, narrowly conceived, offers no reason for voting at all.[3] It seems that people go to the polling station either out of a sense of civic duty or for the satisfaction of recording their own opinions. It does not, therefore, seem implausible to suppose that, when they get there, they sometimes record their beliefs about social welfare. Nor is it implausible to suppose that many people genuinely believe that social welfare is best served by the continued existence of the welfare state.

Even if we reject the hypothesis that we live in a 'caring economy', and assume instead that individuals' preferences are selfish, it is not *illogical* to argue in favour of the welfare state. But we cannot also insist on the liberal principle that each adult is the proper judge of his own welfare and that the welfare of society is no

---

[1] This idea can be found in some of the classic texts of liberal political theory – J. S. Mill, *Considerations on Representative Government*, London, 1861, Ch. 3, for example. Mill argues that participation in politics teaches the individual to 'weigh interests not his own' and to feel an 'unselfish sentiment of identification with the public'.

[2] This is not to deny that the contrary view – that it is perfectly proper to vote according to one's private interests – has its adherents. I am inclined to this view myself.

[3] This conclusion is extremely embarrassing for those economists who are trying to build a 'positive' theory of public choice – that is, a theory of how public choices are made in real life, rather than a theory of how they ought to be made. As one public choice theorist, Professor Dennis Mueller, has admitted, the problem still awaits a satisfactory solution. (D. C. Mueller, *Public Choice*, Cambridge University Press, 1979, pp. 120-124.)

more than the welfare of its individual members. We may support the ideal of the welfare state, as espoused by Titmuss, or the ideal of liberty, as espoused by Mill – but not both.

I shall describe two kinds of argument which can be, and have been, made in support of the welfare state, and I shall suggest that their popularity may help to explain why the welfare state continues to exist.

The paternalist argument for the welfare state

Let us suppose that medical care is not provided or subsidised by the state, but is bought and sold like other commodities. Private companies offer insurance policies which provide cover for medical expenses. Two people, Jones and Williams, reach adulthood in good health, with equal wealth and equal job prospects. Jones chooses to insure while Williams chooses not to. Some years later, both of them contract a serious illness. Jones receives a high standard of medical care, paid for by his insurance company. Williams receives a lower standard of medical care, and to pay for it he has to sacrifice a good deal of his accustomed standard of living. Would it have been better if there had been no choice about insurance and if Williams had been compelled to take out the same kind of insurance policy as Jones did? Supporters of the welfare state would presumably answer: 'Yes'.

One way of justifying an answer of 'Yes' – and, more generally, of justifying the welfare state – is to argue that adults are not always the best judges of their own welfare. We might claim that Williams's decision not to insure is so irrational or imprudent that it would be better for him if he were denied the option of not insuring in the first place. This is a paternalistic argument which runs counter to the spirit of Mill's ideal of individual liberty. It is, however, internally consistent. This kind of argument was often put forward in the 19th century when the foundations of the modern welfare state were being laid down. Thus the emergence of the welfare state, if not of all of its more recent developments, may perhaps be accounted for in terms of paternalistic ideas.

Victorian social policy was founded on, and grew out of, the Poor Law Amendment Act of 1834. Throughout the rest of that century, there was a remarkable consensus of opinion that the 'principles of 1834' were sound. The Act was firmly based on

[35]

utilitarian principles. The Poor Law Commission of 1832, whose Report formed the basis of the Act, included several dedicated Benthamite utilitarians; and its most influential member, Edwin Chadwick, was a utilitarian of the most logical and unsentimental kind. Nineteenth-century utilitarians were not committed to the idea that the individual was necessarily the best judge of his own welfare. How far a person was capable of judging his own interests was considered to be a question of fact, a matter of human psychology rather than doctrine. Utilitarians could be paternalistic. They often suggested that – as Arthur Pigou, the distinguished utilitarian economist of the early 20th century, put it – people have a 'defective telescopic faculty', that is, a tendency to underestimate the true significance to themselves of future events and future sensations. This hypothesis allowed the utilitarians to argue for a social minimum – a level of subsistence below which no-one should be allowed to sink.

One of the fundamental 'principles of 1834' was that people came to the Poor Law for assistance mainly as a result of their own past failings or of the failings of their families. To be in need of relief was to confess to a lack of foresight in the past. Thus, for example, the Report of the 1832 Commission pointed to the amount of savings held by ordinary labourers as evidence that a prudent worker would not need relief.[1] This idea led to the famous principle of 'less eligibility': since to subsidise imprudence would be to encourage it, a person receiving relief should not be in a position 'really or apparently so eligible as the situation of the independent labourer of the lowest class'. But the Commissioners did not conclude that, because (in their view) the very poor were responsible for their own misfortunes, no relief should be given. In the last resort, they should be rescued from the worst consequences of their own folly. This was paternalism.

Many of the later developments in Victorian social policy can be understood in terms of the principle of the social minimum – which itself can be interpreted as a paternalistic principle. Public health measures were seen as part of a policy of providing the social minimum at the least cost to the ratepayer. Chadwick, for example, argued that 'sanitary improvements' would reduce the

[1] M. Bruce, *The Coming of the Welfare State*, 4th edn., Batsford, London, 1968, p. 110.

cost of poor relief since ill-health was a major cause of poverty.[1] Even the principle of compulsory insurance against sickness and unemployment, embodied in the Liberal (but not necessarily liberal) reforms of 1906-14, might be viewed in the same light. If people are imprudent even in a régime of 'less eligibility', compulsory insurance may be a more cost-effective way of providing the social minimum than a non-contributory Poor Law.

20th-century egalitarianism

During this century, a different kind of argument has become increasingly popular as a justification of publicly-financed welfare services. This argument is not paternalistic, but neither is it compatible with the individualistic principles of liberalism. *And it has nothing to do with 'caring'.*

Let me return to my example of Jones who insures against ill-health and Williams who chooses not to. The result is that when Jones falls ill he receives medical care at the expense of his insurance company, whilst when Williams also falls ill he has to endure a lower quality of medical care or a drastic reduction in his standard of living. Some people would say that the inequality between the positions of the two is bad *simply because it is an inequality.* 'In a good society', such people would declare, 'medical care would be allocated according to people's needs; it is wholly wrong that, when two people are in equal need of medical care (that is, when their medical circumstances are the same), one should receive more than the other. Even if this inequality arises out of the free choice of the individuals concerned, it is still an inequality and it is still wrong.'

It is fashionable to use the word 'obscene' when putting forward this kind of argument. Unequal care for people with equal needs is, it is said, an 'obscenity' – a sort of eyesore on the social landscape. The use of this sort of word is significant because it suggests there is a parallel between judgements about the good of society and aesthetic judgements – such as what makes a good painting or a good colour scheme. This is a fundamentally anti-liberal idea.

Liberals usually insist that society is nothing more than the sum of the individuals who make it up, and that the welfare of

[1] M. Bruce, *ibid.,* p. 66.

society is composed of nothing more nor less than the welfare of these individuals. Thus if, as a result of a re-arrangement in society, some people are made better-off without anyone being made worse-off, social welfare (as seen by a liberal) necessarily increases. This is true even if it produces more inequality.

Aesthetic judgements, however, obey a different kind of logic. If I replace the green carpet in my living room with a more beautiful ochre one, and replace the green wallpaper with more beautiful lilac paper, I do not necessarily make the room as a whole more beautiful. In making aesthetic judgements, we do not simply evaluate the component parts of a room or a painting in isolation; we also consider how they stand *in relation to one another*. Similarly, some people believe that we cannot make judgements about the welfare of society merely by considering the welfare of each individual *in isolation*. It also matters how these individuals stand in relation to one another. This idea that society must be judged as a whole may be called *collectivistic*, as opposed to the *individualistic* viewpoint taken by liberals.

There is wide agreement among historians of social policy and of philanthropy that a major change in public opinion occurred around the turn of the century when collectivistic ideas began to gain ascendancy over individualistic ones.[1] Collectivism showed itself in many different forms, not all of which took permanent root in British thinking. One of the more transient – and unpleasant – strands in collectivistic thought was social Darwinism and militarism. For a short period up to the First World War it was fashionable to view the world as a battleground of races and to treat the race, rather than the individual, as the proper unit for moral theories. The poor and the sick tended to be seen not so much as suffering individuals for whom one should feel compassion, but rather as a diseased limb of the racial body requiring treatment in the interests of the whole. The treatments recommended were sometimes rather drastic; progressive socialist thinkers such as George Bernard Shaw and the Webbs were very interested in the possibilities of eugenics.[2] Perhaps surprisingly, these ideas had a lasting influence on the development of social

[1] M. Bruce, *ibid.*, Ch. 5; J. R. Hay, *The Origins of the Liberal Welfare Reforms*, Macmillan, London, 1975; R. Pinker, *The Idea of Welfare*, Heinemann, London, 1979, Ch. 7.
[2] R. Pinker, *ibid.*, p. 100.

policy. As Titmuss pointed out, 'the personal health movement which eventually led to the National Health Service' was 'touched off' not by compassion but by a militaristic concern about the low standards of health among volunteers for the Boer War.[1]

Diversity of liberal values versus *collectivistic principle of fraternity*

A more lasting strand of collectivistic thought emphasises the value of *fraternity* – of a sense of brotherhood or common citizenship between people. The principle of fraternity is collectivistic because it concerns the way in which people stand in relation to one another; in this sense it is anti-liberal. Let us compare two alternative ways of organising a society. Under one, everybody has an income of £5,000 a year. Under the other, half the population get £5,000 a year, the other half £10,000. To adopt the second alternative rather than the first is to benefit some people whilst harming none; an individualist would have to say that this amounted to an increase in social welfare. In contrast, someone who valued fraternity might believe the first alternative to be better because the second would foster feelings of envy and disunity.

Fraternity is most easily generated when the members of a society are united in the pursuit of a common goal. Wars, for example, are often very effective in fostering feelings of common purpose and citizenship – and the same can be said of revolutions. The 'spirit of 1940' is a British cliché, but it expresses a genuine and deeply-felt emotion – which has recently re-asserted itself as the 'Falklands factor'. Many historians have suggested that the wartime experience of national unity was an important cause of the widespread public support for the welfare policies of Clement Attlee's Labour Government. This suggests another reason why fraternity cannot be regarded as a liberal principle. Liberals emphasise the *diversity* of people's interests and opinions. They reject the common idea that, in a truly good society, there would be no conflicts of interest or opinion and everyone would be united behind a single conception of the social good. As Sir Isaiah Berlin has vigorously argued, this idea is a dangerous

[1] R. M. Titmuss, *Essays on 'the Welfare State'*, Allen and Unwin, London, 1958, p. 80.

[39]

illusion, and one which can open the way to tyranny and oppression.[1] To this extent, therefore, liberals must renounce fraternity; 'social unity', in the sense of a unity of purpose, cannot be a liberal value.

Many defences of the welfare state appeal to the value of fraternity. In recommending the scheme of 'social insurance' which became the model for later legislation, William Beveridge wrote in 1942 that this idea

'implies a pooling of risk. . . . The term "social insurance" to describe this institution implies both that it is compulsory and that *men should stand together with their fellows*'.[2]

In a similar vein, Titmuss argued that 'the Health Service is not socially divisive' and that

'One of the principles of the National Blood Transfusion Service and the National Health Service is to provide services on the basis of common human needs; *there must be no allocation of resources which could create a sense of separateness between people*.'[3]

Since I have plundered Professor Maurice Bruce's book, *The Coming of the Welfare State*, so shamelessly in search of quotations, I shall let him have a word himself. Occasionally, Bruce the historian gives way to Bruce the citizen, and citizen Bruce is in no doubt that the coming of the welfare state was a good thing. Referring to the social reforms carried out during and immediately after the Second World War, he writes:

'The war speeded changes and left a country . . . markedly more humane and civilised than that of 1939 . . . with a degree of unity and equality far beyond what had previously been possible . . . What gave the social legislation its appeal was above all its universality, the universality that was itself a reflection of war-time unity.'[4]

In each of these three quotations the welfare state is defended on the ground that it fosters feelings of common citizenship

---

[1] I. Berlin, *Four Essays on Liberty*, Oxford University Press, 1969.

[2] W. H. Beveridge, *Social Insurance and Allied Services*, HMSO, London, 1942, para. 26 (emphasis added).

[3] R. M. Titmuss, *The Gift Relationship*, op. cit., p. 255 and p. 268 (emphasis added).

[4] M. Bruce, *op. cit.*, p. 326.

between people. Beveridge and Titmuss were both quite explicit that such feelings ought to be fostered. Titmuss also said (or implied very strongly) that to provide health services according to any criterion other than medical need is to create feelings of 'separateness', which is the opposite of fraternity. Bruce is less explicit, but the same ideas come through. He clearly attaches value to the feelings of unity engendered by war, and regards such feelings as a mark of a 'civilised' society.

Fraternal opposition to safety-net welfare

The principle of fraternity can be used to support a comprehensive or 'universal' system of welfare services, in contrast to the safety-net approach that can be justified on paternalistic grounds. To anyone whose values are individualistic, it is natural that social arrangements should reflect the diversity of people's interests and preferences. That different people should consume different bundles of goods and services is entirely right and proper. But someone whose values are collectivistic is not committed to this conclusion. Once it is accepted that social unity is a good thing in its own right, and that a 'sense of separateness' is bad, it becomes natural to say that conformity is good, that people in like circumstances ought to consume the same combinations of goods and services whether they would choose to do so or not.

The idea that publicly-financed welfare services should form no more than a safety-net can thus be opposed by an appeal to the principle of fraternity. The mere existence of diversity can be interpreted as an affront to this principle. Some collectivists therefore not only argue for the public provision of a high (rather than a minimum) standard of welfare services; they also maintain that no-one ought to enjoy higher standards than others, even if he is willing to pay for them by sacrificing goods he considers less important. It is impossible to understand the intensity of feeling aroused by recent debates about 'pay beds' in NHS hospitals, or about the role of private schools in the education system, without recognising that many people sincerely believe that a private sector in these services is wrong in principle. For such people, equality of outcome – and not equality of opportunity or freedom of choice – is of overriding value. In his recent book

[41]

The Politics of Procrustes, Professor Antony Flew has documented just how widespread is the attachment to equality for its own sake.[1]

It might be thought that this emphasis on the value of fraternity is no more than a debating ploy on the part of the welfare state's ideologues. But the principle of allocation according to need is deeply embedded in many of the institutions of the welfare state. Here is one example. The NHS has to ration medical care; decisions have to be made about which of a group of patients should be treated first. Let us suppose – as is sometimes the case – that patients are unable to work until they have received treatment. What system of rationing should be used? Any rationing system is likely to depend on a combination of criteria, such as giving priority to people in most discomfort or who have waited longest. But should *one* of the criteria be that patients with higher earnings get priority?

There is a good argument, on grounds of economic efficiency, for taking some account of a patient's potential earnings. More highly paid workers contribute more in taxes while they are working, and so taxpayers as a whole benefit if better-paid workers return to work more quickly.[2] At least one prominent health economist, Professor Alan Williams, has been brave enough to face up to this conclusion. It would, he says, be 'perversely masochistic' not to take account of potential earnings when determining priorities in the NHS.[3] In practice, however, this is not what happens. The very suggestion that patients with higher potential earnings should receive priority would be thought heretical – because it violates the principle that the allocation of medical care should be according to need *and need alone*. Although the suggestion cannot be faulted on individualistic grounds, it contravenes a collectivistic principle of equality or fraternity.

[1] A. Flew, *The Politics of Procrustes: Contradictions of Enforced Equality*, Prometheus Books, Buffalo, NY, 1981.

[2] Incidentally, this argument would apply even in a 'caring economy' where everyone was concerned about everyone else's health care. All that is being assumed is that, other things equal, people prefer lower taxes to higher taxes.

[3] The quotation is from an unpublished paper presented by Professor Williams to a Health Economists' Study Group meeting in York in 1979.

VII

THE CONTINUING DEBATE

ECONOMISTS WHO write about public policy are usually expected to demonstrate the usefulness of their work by producing recommendations that government might act on. In the jargon of economics, a piece of work is not regarded as practical or useful unless it leads to some 'policy implications'. Many readers, I imagine, will want to know what policies I am recommending – and will perhaps feel cheated by my answer, which is 'None'.

The idea that economists can make professional pronouncements about what government ought and ought not to do presupposes that some fundamental political or moral principles are uncontroversial. The economist is no better qualified than anyone else to say what the *ultimate* objectives of government should be; all he or she can say is that, *if* government wants to achieve a certain objective, the best way for it to do so is to adopt a particular policy. If people do not agree about ultimate objectives, if they have different ideas about the social good, it may be impossible for the economist to present a 'neutral' or 'professional' recommendation. That is not the fault of economics or economists; it is simply the way the world is.

I have argued that the welfare state is one of those issues on which ultimate values come into conflict. The principle of liberty, as expounded by John Stuart Mill, states that society should not impose restrictions on an individual unless they are necessary *to prevent harm to other individuals.* According to this principle, it is wrong to compel people to save for old age, or to insure against ill-health or unemployment, as a means of protecting them from harming *themselves.* We may feel convinced that the person who fails to save or insure is making a grave mistake which he or she will later regret. If, however, we use this as an argument for compulsory saving or insuring, we are being paternalistic: we are not acknowledging the right of the individual to plan his or her own life. It is also contrary to the principle of liberty to impose restrictions on an individual as a means of bringing about some desired *pattern* of consumption among individuals. We may believe that, in a truly good or civilised society, medical care would be allocated according to medical need. But if we try to

[43]

bring about such an allocation by compelling people to take out health insurance – or by preventing them from buying more health care than other people – we are pursuing equality or fraternity at the expense of liberty.

The welfare state is, among other things, a system of compulsory insurance and compulsory saving. To this extent, at least, every major Western country is a welfare state. The USA, for example, has tax-financed retirement pensions and social security payments, and a hospital insurance scheme (Medicare) which is compulsory for certain classes of people. Whatever the benefits of these arrangements – and there are many – it remains true that they have been bought at a price. Liberty has been sacrificed.

The 'caring economy' explanation of the welfare state denies that this price has been paid at all. According to that explanation, the compulsion which lies behind the welfare state is not what it seems. The person who refuses to insure himself is harming *other people*, because they care about his consumption of health services or about his standard of living when he is old. Thus, we are told, compulsory insurance and saving schemes are no more paternalistic than a law against drunken driving. I have tried to show that this argument is mistaken. First, because it rests on a theory of charitable behaviour which is plainly inconsistent with the evidence of private philanthropy and voluntary social service. Secondly, because it fails to take account of the emphasis that the founders and upholders of the welfare state have placed on paternalistic and egalitarian arguments.

Thinking clearly about social policy

Does all this really matter? No-one – not even such an advocate of the free market as Professor Friedman – seriously proposes the abolition of all elements of compulsory saving for old age and compulsory insurance against ill-health. Everyone, it seems, favours at least some kind of safety-net social policy. So is there any point in asking whether the arguments which people use to justify such a policy are internally consistent? I think there is.

The most fundamental reason I can give is one John Stuart Mill put forward in *On Liberty*. The popularity of a belief, or the certainty with which we hold it, he wrote, is never a reason for refusing to question it:

'However unwillingly a person who has a strong opinion may admit the possibility that his opinion may be false, he ought to be moved by the consideration that, however true it may be, if it is not fully, frequently, and fearlessly discussed, it will be held as a dead dogma, not a living truth.'[1]

No thinking person ought to be satisfied with holding an opinion he or she does not know how to defend – even if everyone else shares that opinion. There is still less reason to be satisfied with a *false* 'justification' for a popular opinion.

The wholesale abolition of the welfare state is not on the political agenda; but the proper extent of its functions is a matter of continuing debate. Strong passions are aroused about whether the welfare state should be 'universal' or 'selective' and about the role of the private sector in medical care and education. Our attitudes to these issues are influenced by our ideas about how the uncontroversial parts of the welfare state are justified. If we cannot think clearly about the fundamental question, 'Why do we have *any* kind of social policy?', we are unlikely to think clearly about the more controversial questions.

Most people, even the most committed collectivists, have some residual liberal inclinations; most of us value individual freedom. And almost everyone recognises the desirability of at least a safety-net social policy. What I am saying is that we ought to be honest about the tension between these two commitments. Those who wholeheartedly support the idea of an extensive welfare state ought to recognise the cost in terms of individual freedom. Those who, like Professor Friedman, use arguments about freedom to justify rolling back the frontiers of the welfare state ought to admit that they too are sometimes prepared to sacrifice freedom for other – possibly paternalistic – values. We should not pretend that this moral conflict does not exist.

[1] J. S. Mill, *On Liberty*, Ch. 2.

[45]

SOME IEA PAPERS ON WELFARE

Readings 12

The Economics of Charity

Essays on the comparative economics and ethics of giving and selling, with applications to blood

ARMEN ALCHIAN, WILLIAM ALLEN, MICHAEL COOPER, ANTHONY CULYER, MARILYN IRELAND, THOMAS IRELAND, DAVID JOHNSON, JAMES KOCH, A. J. SALSBURY, GORDON TULLOCK

1974   xviii + 197 pp   £2.00

'The first paper is concerned with the utility derived from charitable activities; the second with the politics of the redistribution of benefits in society; the third, fourth and fifth with the anthropology, ethics, and welfare economics, respectively, of "giving" . . . The second part deals with the application of such a framework to blood transfusion. The best paper in the whole selection is by Culyer and Cooper on the economics of giving and selling blood: an attempt to refute Titmuss's arguments.'

D. Jackson, *Economic Journal*

'. . . a most valuable contribution to the debate.'

A. J. B. Rowe, *Social & Economic Administration*

Research Monograph 37

The Moral Hazard of Social Benefits

A study of the impact of social benefits and income tax on incentives to work

HERMIONE PARKER

1982   £3.00

'Every politician should read it for the devastating evidence it provides.'   Ronald Butt, *The Times*

'Mrs Hermione Parker demonstrates persuasively in a monograph published today by the Institute of Economic Affairs that 5·5 million people, or 20 per cent of the workforce, are now close enough to the unemployment and poverty traps for their morale and motivation to be affected.'   *Financial Times*, in an Editorial

Hobart Paper 73
Poverty before Politics
A proposal for a Reverse Income Tax
COLIN CLARK
1977 £1.50
'. . . our present tax and welfare arrangements do not in any adequate way provide for this kind of redistribution [minimum income]. Everyone's grateful thanks, therefore, ought to go to Professor Colin Clark and the Institute of Economic Affairs for publishing a pamphlet which draws attention to this and suggests the shape of what ought to be done.'

Anthony Harris, *Financial Times*

Occasional Paper 60
Wither the Welfare State
ARTHUR SELDON
1981 £1.50
'Recent developments seem to be lending support to a thesis which Arthur Seldon . . . has been propounding for many years, namely that the British welfare state will meet increasing strains in the attempt to perpetuate itself in the face of market forces which conflict with it. Growing resistance to rate rises on the one hand and the spread of private welfare services, such as health insurance, on the other do indeed suggest that there is a limit beyond which people are no longer prepared to pay more taxes for services which offer them no choice.'   *Banker*

Hobart Paper 41
The Price of Blood
MICHAEL COOPER and ANTHONY CULYER
1968 50p
'A crisis in the supply of blood in the foreseeable future is envisaged by two economists from Exeter University. They suggest that one way of averting the crisis, and more particularly stopping the wastage of blood, would be to offer donors £2 per session. The economists . . . calculate that even in an unpaid donor system, expenses, including those incurred in promotion and advertising, raise the marginal cost of a pint of blood to between £4 and £5. They argue that demand and supply of blood can be analysed by economists in much the same way as guns, butter or lettuce.'

Guardian

[47]

Hobart Paperback 13

Over-Ruled on Welfare

A 15-year investigation into private preferences and public policy based on surveys in 1963, 1965, 1970, 1978 into priced choice between state and private services

RALPH HARRIS and ARTHUR SELDON

1979   xxx + 250 pp   £3.00

'The Government's steps towards greater freedom of choice through lower taxation, one of the main planks of its election platform, has received massive endorsement from a new survey by the Institute of Economic Affairs.'

Desmond Quigley, *Financial Times*

'. . . the ideas adumbrated so readably in this book do have most plausible application. . . . the IEA's splendidly anti-bureaucratic principles are an invaluable antidote to public sector Toryism as much as socialism.'   *Economist*

Occasional Paper 63

**The Welfare State:
For Rich or for Poor?**

DAVID G. GREEN

1982   £1.20

'The middle classes often do better out of the Welfare State than the poor for whom it was intended . . . the middle classes are frequently chief beneficiaries of many State welfare handouts, even though these are paid for to a large extent by taxes on the less well-off.'   *Daily Telegraph*

'The Welfare State is failing the low-paid people it was designed to help and should be scrapped. . . . Former Labour Councillor Dr David Green claims middle class people do better out of the system.

'Dr Green, now a research fellow at an Australian university, says that middle-class people tend to benefit more because they know how to manipulate the system in their own interests.'

Daily Mail